HUMMINGBIRDS

HUMMINGBIRDS

Mark J. Rauzon

A First Book

FRANKLIN WATTS   *A Division of Grolier Publishing*
New York • London • Hong Kong • Sydney • Danbury, Connecticut

Frontispiece: A broad-billed hummingbird feeds from a flower.
Photo credits ©: Animals Animals: 25 (G. I. Bernard),
49 (E. R. Degginger), 22, 33, 39 (Michael Fogden), 44 (Mickey Gibson),
46 (Dr. F. Koster/Survival Oxford Scientific Films), 18 (Bates Littlehales),
17 (Joe McDonald), 54 (Oxford Scientific Films), 14 (Maresa Pryor),
53 (Jack Wilburn); Hugh P. Smith, Jr.: 21, 40, 57; John Gilanti: 34;
Mark J. Rauzon: 50; Peter Arnold Inc.: 43 (Kevin Schaffer), 13 (G. Ziesler);
Photo Researchers: cover (Peter Arnold); VIREO: 26 (Doug Weschler),
31 (C. H. Greenwalt); Visuals Unlimited: 29, 37 (S. Maslowski),
2 (Joe McDonald), 59 (J. Serrao), 10 (Laurel Wallace).

Library of Congress Cataloging-in-Publication Data

Rauzon, Mark J.
Hummingbirds / Mark J. Rauzon. — 1st ed.
p. cm. — (A First book)
Includes bibliographical references (p.   ) and index.
Summary: Describes the physical characteristics, behavior,
and habitat of the smallest bird in the world.
ISBN 0-531-20260-7 (lib.bdg.)   0-531-15849-7 (pbk.)
1. Hummingbirds—Juvenile literature. [1. Hummingbirds.]
I. Title. II. Series.
QL696.A558R38 1997
598.8'99—DC20
                                                    96-36156
                                                        CIP
                                                         AC

To my niece,
Ava Carmody

CONTENTS

HUMMINGBIRDS

A hummer gets dinner on the fly.

HUNGRY, HOVERING HUMMERS

Hummingbirds are the bees of the bird world, busily buzzing from flower to flower. Sipping sweet nectar with needlelike bills and long, flexible tongues, these tiny birds seem always to be on the move, zipping by in a blur in search of sweet-nectar jet fuel for their rapid flight.

Hummingbirds, or hummers as they are called for short, are some of nature's most amazing creatures. The smallest birds in the world, hummingbirds have the fewest feathers, the fastest wing beats, and the biggest appetites. These frail-looking birds give the impression of extraordinary power packed into a tiny bundle. They do nothing in slow motion. Their wings have only one speed—very fast.

By beating their wings as many as eighty times per second, hummingbirds can fly forward, backward, sideways, and even upside down. They can also hover motionless except for their vibrating wings. The family name of hummingbirds, Trochilidae, comes from the Greek word for wheel, and indeed their blurred wings look like a spinning circle of spokes.

The hummingbird's unique ability to fly comes from its internal bone structure. Instead of folding like other bird wings, the hummingbird's wings are rigid from shoulder to tip. Hummers rotate their short, narrow wings from their shoulders in figure eights and twist and turn their wings so they are pushing on the air with each stoke. Most birds fly with the wings providing power on the downstroke only. The ten wing feathers of the hummers vibrate on the upstroke and downstroke, causing their wings to hum. The noises that their wings make sound different for every kind, or species, of hummer.

The giant hummingbird is the largest hummingbird species. It is $8\frac{1}{2}$ inches (22 cm) long, about the size of a starling. Found in the Andes Mountains of South America, the giant hummer beats its wings at eight to ten beats per second, which is average for most small birds. Other hummers have been clocked at 200 beats

A giant hummingbird nests on a Peruvian cactus.

per second, while bees buzz at 250 times a second and mosquitoes whine at 600 times a second!

The smallest bird in the world is the bee hummingbird from Cuba. It is about 2 inches (5 cm) long,

Hummingbirds have to fuel in flight to sustain their energetic activity.

including its bill and tail. The average hummer is about 3 to 4 inches (8 to 10 cm) long and weighs about as much as a nickel.

The tiny hummingbirds get cold more quickly than larger animals because there is less mass to hold their body heat. Hummingbird body temperatures are between 105°F (41°C) and 110°F (43°C), which is warmer than those of larger animals. Compared to all other animals, the hummingbird has a heart that is bigger in relative proportion to its size. Its heart beats up to twelve hundred beats per minute when the hummer is flying and five hundred beats per minute when it is resting. In order to sustain themselves at this pace, hummers must turn food into energy faster than bigger animals.

Hummingbirds burn energy at an extremely rapid rate. They require easily digested sugars, which pass right into the bloodstream. Within minutes, the energy in the food is used, waste moves through the system, and the hummer needs more food. Hummingbirds must consume half their weight daily to stay alive. This requires visiting more than a thousand blossoms a day! Hummers must find food every ten to fifteen minutes in order to sustain themselves and their frantic flight.

When sipping nectar, the birds hover right in front of the flower. Usually there is no landing pad but whenever they can find a perch to sit and sip, they do. Sunangels feed by clinging to a flower with their wings outstretched in a **V**.

Hummingbirds cannot live on nectar alone. They also eat insects to get protein. They probe flowers and the undersides of leaves, gleaning insects from tree trunks, and catch flies during flight. They even steal captured insects out of spiderwebs and then eat the spiders, too. However, most of their food is nectar.

Hummingbirds are always looking for ways to save their energy. Although they seem always to be on the move, they rest during much of day and all of the night. At night, some hummers save energy by lowering their body temperatures and heart rate. This process is known as torpor when it lasts for a brief time and as hibernation when it extends over a long period. Many hummers live high in the mountains, where after the sun sets, temperatures drop to near freezing in the thin air. They fluff up their feathers, lower their heart rate, and go to sleep. When they wake up, they cannot fly. It takes about ten minutes to increase their metabolism— the ability to make food into energy for the body to use—and warm up their wings.

Hummingbirds will at times sit quietly perched,
sometimes entering a state called torpor to save energy.

If hummingbirds had to maintain their body temperature at 105°F (41°C) all the time, they might run out of energy during the night and freeze to death. Torpor is useful when bad weather sets in and hummers can't get out to the flowers for fuel. When the sun comes out and warms up the day, hummers go back to work on their endless quest for food.

The hummingbirds that migrate must build up fat reserves to burn when they fly. One of the most familiar species, the ruby-throated hummingbird, holds the record for flight endurance. During migration from their wintering grounds in Mexico to their summer homes in eastern North America, they fly nonstop across 500 miles (805 km) of the Gulf of Mexico at 30 miles (48 km) per hour. It takes about 14½ hours of nonstop flying, beating its wings 4,200 times per minute and 252,000 times per hour (over 4 million beats in all), to cross the ocean!

Before migrating nonstop across the Gulf of Mexico, the ruby-throated hummingbird increases its body weight almost 50 percent.

The rufous hummingbird migrates thousands of miles during a year but makes many stops to feed along the way. Other hummers migrate up and down mountains as spring changes to summer and then to fall. They are always looking for flowering trees and plants in a wide variety of climates from near-freezing mountaintops to hot jungles.

Hummingbirds are always hungry. Maybe that's why they are so aggressive. Their quarrelsome personalities are necessary to defend their food sources from other hummingbirds. Sky battles often erupt when one hummer invades another's territory, usually a patch of red flowers. The invader is speedily chased away with a chattering, scolding, "zeee-chuppity-chup-chup." Sometimes, two hummers lock bills and flutter to the ground, neither wanting to give up the fight.

Hummers dive at other birds and dragonflies to chase them out of their territory. In the air they are more maneuverable than larger birds, so hummers are able to chase even hawks away. A hawk cannot turn fast or sharp enough to catch an annoying hummer. But yellow jacket wasps are able to chase hummers away from sugar water feeders. Whether hummers ever get stung is unknown. Moths known as

Two male Anna's hummingbirds fight over territory.

Taking a break from hovering,
this green-crowned brilliant perches on a branch.

hummingbird hawkmoths hover just like hummers, sipping the flowers' sweet nectar.

Hummingbirds are related to swifts, birds that are said to look like flying cigars. Swifts soar at 100 miles (161 km) per hour on stiff wings, alternating with twinkling wing beats. While hummers can stop on a dime, swifts must fly in circles to stop. They both have weak feet and must land on perches for they are helpless on the ground. They can't jump, hop, or walk. They can only fly. One exception is the rainbow-bearded thornbill, a hummingbird that is able to walk on flattened mats of grass looking for insects.

On the ground, hummingbirds are vulnerable to being caught and eaten by larger birds such as jays and hawks. They can get caught by praying mantises and frogs as well as in spiderwebs and on the barbs of sticky plants. Predators like opossums, snakes, lizards, and other birds are always looking out for hummingbird eggs to eat and will rob any nest they can find. In the rain forests of Costa Rica, yellow eyelash vipers wait next to flowers for hummers to visit. They may even be investigated by hummers looking for flowers. In the instant blink of an eye, the viper can strike and catch a bird.

Inspiration Through the Ages

Few animals have captured people's imaginations as much as hummingbirds have. They have inspired poets such as John Keats and Emily Dickinson to sing their praises, artists such as John James Audubon and John Gould to draw and paint them, gardeners to plant flowers for hummers, and environmentalists to protect rain forests for them.

Thousands of years ago, in the deserts along the coast of Peru, ancient Incan people drew 200-foot- (61-m-) long images of hummingbirds in the sand. Native Americans believed that hummingbird feathers held magical powers. When hummingbirds were first brought to Europe, an immediate desire for their precious feathers developed. Bird trappers collected hummers in the

This 1812 illustration shows the popularity of hummingbirds throughout the ages.

remote mountains of the Americas. When they sent specimens back to be made into jewelry, scientists were able to identify the wonderful bird skins. They could scarcely believe such exquisite creatures existed.

The beauty and splendor of hummingbirds almost defies description. Scientists did their best in trying to name them. Their efforts evoke a magical world where knights clad in shining armor fly forth with their swords ready to do battle. It's easy to imagine bronze-tailed plumeleteers, rainbow-bearded thornbills, and bearded helmetcrests as brave young warriors who set out to save the crowned wood-nymphs, festive coquettes, violet-tailed sylphs, and amethyst woodstars from the evil hoary pufflegs and green hermits. During a terrific war, saberwings, sunangels, purple-crowned fairies, and shining sunbeams would come to their aid. For their reward, the empress brilliant might present them with coppery emeralds, golden-tailed sapphires, and fiery topaz, and they would live happily ever after with mountain velvetbreasts, sparkling violet-ears, golden-bellied starfrontlets, and velvet-purple coronets.

Some hummingbirds were named to honor famous people. Anna's hummingbird is named for the Duchess

This empress brilliant sits on her throne in the forest.

Anna Rivoli, the wife of the European duke Rivoli, who lived from 1806 to 1896. He had a hummer named after him until recently. Rivoli's hummingbird is now called the magnificent hummingbird. Other hummers named after people have been retitled with more descriptive names. Prevost's hummingbird is now the green-breasted mango and Dupont's hummingbird is now the sparkling-tailed hummer.

Hummingbirds are living jewels sparkling in the sunlight. John James Audubon called them "glittering fragments of the rainbow." Special types of feathers catch the sunlight and reflect it back in brilliant, iridescent colors. Unlike other birds, whose feathers contain pigments or chemical colors, the hummingbird's feathers use the properties of light to show color. If the light does not strike their plumage, they may look dark and be almost impossible to identify. Although all of them are mostly green and brown on their backs, sunlight sparkling on hot pink or dazzling purple feathers distinguishes them. When they turn and catch the light on their throat feathers, called the gorget, they shine like sequins that change from green to orange glittery to a fiery red. In addition to their gorgeous gorget, some have crests, fan-shaped ruffs, and long mustaches.

Catching the light, the iridescent feathers of an
Anna's hummingbird flash a strawberry red.

Despite their beauty, hummingbirds lack musical ability. Voice is less important for these birds. Generally, the drab birds are the accomplished songsters. Only a few species, like Anna's hummingbirds, even attempt to sing a song and then it's a jumble of squeaky notes repeated over and over. Hummers also utter high-pitched call notes that are given frequently while feeding. Their wings and tails make distinct whistles and whines, especially when they engage in spectacular flight displays.

The males use their unique flying ability to impress the females. They do aerial acrobatic flight displays. Most impressive is the power dive of the male Anna's hummingbird. He shoots straight up to 150 feet (46 m) over the female. At the highest point of his flight, he is barely visible from the ground. Out of the blue, he plummets head first at 60 miles (96 km) per hour by the perched female and makes a loud metallic-sounding pop with his tail feathers. An instant later, he helicopters straight up again and continues to dive out of the sky repeating the display several times.

Although most hummers have ten tail feathers, the spatulate-tailed hummingbird has only four tail feathers. The outer two look like flexible badminton rackets with extra long handles. The male whips them together over his head to draw attention to himself. Sometimes,

Spatulate-tailed hummingbirds have four elongated
tail feathers that they show off during courtship.

several males take part in the display. As they jump,
their tail feathers make clicking noises together.

The red-billed streamertail has the longest tail of any
hummer. This spectacular 10-inch (25-cm) bird flutters
and rustles its tail when it flies. It is Jamaica's national bird
and is known as the doctorbird because it seems to have
the same black coattails that doctors wore in the 1800s.

BILLS FOR FEEDING

Hummingbird bills have adapted to fit specific kinds of flowers. President Theodore Roosevelt once noticed this phenomenon during an expedition in Brazil. He observed that the sickle-billed hummingbird's strongly curved bill was adapted specifically for the blossoms of marsh plants and that these birds never fed from any other plants.

Hummingbird bills can differ greatly in shape and length. The tooth-billed hummer has a serrated bill, jagged like a steak knife. It saws open the bottom of flowers as a shortcut to get to the sweet pot of nectar. The sword-billed hummingbird is the only bird with a bill that is longer than its body. This hummer must tip its 4-inch (10-cm) bill up to balance the load when it

The matching contours of the white-tipped sickle-billed hummingbird's bill and the heliconia flower suggest that the bird and plant evolved together.

When a hummingbird gleans nectar from the inside of a flower, pollen accumulates on its bill.

rests. The mountain avocetbill is the only hummer with an upturned bill. It is named after a shorebird called the avocet, which has a long, upswept beak.

Hummingbirds use their needlelike bills and long tongues in combination to feed. After they insert their thin bills in flowers, their fringe-tipped tongues flick in and out until the flower is empty of nectar. Like long, thin straws that are slightly forked at the tip, hummingbird tongues are specialized for feeding from flowers. They lick up nectar and any small insects that may be there. The hummer will return when the flower is full of nectar again and may defend it from other "nectar rustlers."

Flowering plants benefit from hummingbirds. Plants cannot make seeds unless they are pollinated, or fertilized, so flowers have evolved lures to attract pollinators. Up to 50 percent of flowers need hummingbirds to pollinate them. Plants that use hummers as pollinators have red or orange tube-shaped flowers with lots of sweet nectar and little scent. Hummers have a poor sense of smell but they see in color. Brightly colored flowers are visited more often than less colorful ones. In fact, curious hummers have sometimes been known to visit people wearing red.

When hummers feed from deep-throated flowers, they get dusted with pollen. When they visit another flower, the pollen gets mixed together and the flowers become fertilized. Hummers also pick up special hitch-hikers. Almost invisible mites, which are relatives of spiders and ticks, also eat pollen and nectar. They climb aboard the hummingbird's bills and catch a free ride from one source of food to another.

The fiery-throated hummingbird of Costa Rica feeds on a variety of flowering trees. When long, tubular flowers are in bloom, the fiery-throats follow another bird called the slaty flower-piercer. With a beak shaped like pruning shears, slaty flower-piecers cut open the bottom of the blossom to get to the sweets. Fiery-throats follow them and lick their long tongues into blossoms that they could not otherwise reach.

In the breeding season, the male fiery-throat pro-tects a clump of especially sweet flowers by chasing away all intruders except female hummers. The male fiery-throat will permit only his mate to drink from these flowers to guarantee a supply of nectar to raise their young. Even he himself will not drink from these food sources.

Long-tailed hermit hummingbirds have a curved bill designed for probing into heliconias, red flowers related

After feeding at one flower, hummingbirds carry pollen on their bills to the next flower, which helps plants reproduce.

A long-tailed hermit feeds from a heliconia flower.

to bananas and found in the rain forests of Central and South America. The hermits follow a pattern each day, visiting the same flowers in a certain order. This system gives the flower time to make more nectar by the time the hermit returns. Hermits defend these flowers from other hummers who might steal their food.

Hermits live in dense tropical forests and are drab compared to other hummingbirds. Though mainly brown and white, they are still pretty. You can get a close look at hermits because they have a habit of zooming right up to your face as you walk in the forests and examining you at close range before abruptly zooming off into the shadows again.

A female broad-tailed hummingbird sits on a lichen-covered nest in a well-camouflaged spot.

HOME ON THE NEST

Hermit hummingbirds congregate along open spaces near streams. Males perch on low branches and display together. The females are attracted to the areas called "leks," where males sing and wag their tails. Females mate with the males that perform best. Males may visit a lek all year to practice their song and dance routines. When they are not dancing or resting, they are darting from flower to flower or bathing in moving streams and rainstorms.

Male hummers take no part in the nesting effort. After a brief courtship and mating, the male darts off to defend his flowers, while the female goes off to build a nest. Unlike the colorful male, the female has drab coloring. This coloration protects her during the time she must sit on the nest and raise her young, which she does by herself.

Female hummingbirds build a nest from cobwebs, bark, and bits of plant fluff and a flat, rootless plant called lichen. They use sticky spiderwebs to tie the nest together and often saddle a nest on a limb over water for easy access. They use the spiderwebs to attach the nest to the twigs, fill the snug nest bowl with downy feathers, and camouflage the outside with living lichen. In the dark underlying vegetation of the forest called understory, the nest is difficult to find.

Female hermit hummers weave a nest of plant fibers on the underside of a palm, banana, or heliconia leaf. The nest swings in the wind like a suspension bridge. She must dart into the nest and sit facing into the leaf to incubate her tiny eggs. The eggs are visible through the loosely woven fibers, which are just strong enough to support the mother's weight. The female Napo hummingbird, on the other hand, constructs her nest low to the ground on a shrub with broad leaves so she has a roof over her head.

A long-tailed hermit incubates her eggs in a nest tucked into the underside of a leaf.

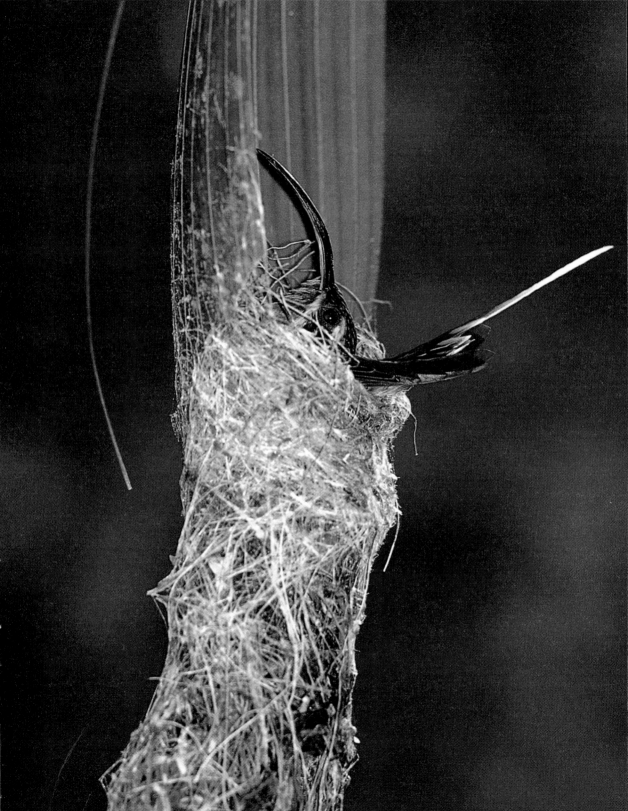

The female hummingbird lays two white eggs no bigger than a thumbnail. They are the smallest bird eggs, about ½ inch (13 mm) long. While they may be small compared to other bird eggs, they are large for the tiny female to lay, for they weigh almost one quarter of her weight.

It is now that the female's drab coloring comes into play. She is hard to notice on the nest as she incubates the eggs for about fourteen days, until the young are ready to hatch. The chicks break out of the eggs by scraping the inside of the shell with their egg tooth—a hard, white, baby tooth at the end of their bill. They scrape until they crack the eggshell and wiggle out of it.

The chicks complete the hatching process without any help from their mother. But the featherless chicks are exhausted after hatching and the female must brood them under her feathers to keep them safe and warm.

At hatching, the young are the size of honeybees. For the first week of life, they are blind, but by the second week, they can see well. During this period their downy feathers grow out and they are able to keep

Hummingbird eggs are the smallest of all bird eggs.

themselves warm. The female feeds them a mixture of nectar and insects. When the chicks beg for food, she inserts her bill down their throats and regurgitates— brings up partially digested food—into their stomachs.

The young "sword-swallowers" grow up quickly. In three and a half weeks they are on their own and the female may lay another set of eggs. Female hummers are very attentive and seldom abandon their eggs or young. If the eggs are lost to predators early in the nesting season, she will lay again.

A mother hummingbird feeds her chicks by inserting her bill down their throats.

HOME
IN THE
AMERICAS

Hummingbirds are found only on the continents of North and South America, which is also known as the Western Hemisphere and the New World. They occur from the tip of Argentina to southern Alaska and on the islands of Cuba and Jamaica.

However, hummingbird look-alikes called sunbirds can be found in the Old World of Africa and Asia. There are about one hundred species of these metallic-colored birds. They flit from flower to flower to sip nectar, but it is only the hummers that can hover in front of the blossoms, suspended in midair, their wings blurring like airplane propellers in motion.

Hummers are essentially tropical birds that venture north to take advantage of summer flowers. The closer

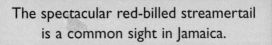
The spectacular red-billed streamertail
is a common sight in Jamaica.

With his long beak working like a giant, single-toothed comb,
this Costa's hummingbird preens every feather into place.

you get to the equator, the more hummingbird species you'll find. For example, one species breeds in Alaska, five in Canada, and twelve in the continental United States. In the vast country of Mexico, there are fifty species, while farther south in the small country of Panama, there are fifty-two species. The center of abundance for hummingbirds, and many other bird species, is Colombia, where there are 143 species—more species than any other country. There are many habitats available in tropical Colombia, since it is on the equator in the Andes Mountains.

Each species of hummingbird prefers a specific breeding habitat, from tropical valleys to mountain ranges. About 340 species of hummingbirds exist in the New World. Occasionally, some species do crossbreed, or hybridize, creating a unique offspring.

In the United States, seven species are common along the Pacific Coast. Allen's, Anna's, and Costa's hummingbirds are common in California and visit bird feeders in people's backyards.

Anna's hummingbird is 3 to 4 inches (8 to 10 cm) long, including the bill. The bright, rose-colored head and neck of the male Anna's is one of the first signs of spring. They are the earliest nesting bird in California and eggs have been recorded as early as December. They live in California all year.

Allen's hummingbird flashes its flaming orange-gold gorget as it zips around the chaparral—a dense growth of low shrubs—in coastal California, usually chased by an Anna's hummer. They spend the winter in Mexico, as do most species of North American hummers.

Costa's hummingbird lives in the Southwest deserts sipping sweet juices from cactus flowers. With its small body, a big, iridescent-purple gorget that looks a handlebar mustache, and ornery nature, Costa's hummers resemble Yosemite Sam, the cartoon character famous for his run-ins with Bugs Bunny.

Smaller still is the calliope hummingbird, the smallest bird in North America. Calliope hummingbirds are almost half the size of Anna's hummers. In spring they return to California from Mexico and move up the mountains as the winter snows melt and the summer flowers bloom. As fall approaches, they leave the high mountains and migrate back to Mexico.

> Some say that Costa's hummingbird, with its handlebar-mustache gorget, looks like the cartoon character Yosemite Sam.

Rufous hummingbirds, which are the northernmost hummingbirds, are marathon migrators.

Some hummers migrate up and down the mountains as the seasons change throughout the year. Other migrate long distances. The ruby-throated hummingbird is the only hummer in the eastern United States and Canada. The area east of the Mississippi is far from the hummingbird center, so they must either cross the vast Gulf of Mexico or travel over areas with few hummingbird flowers. Ruby-throats are few and far between in the eastern portion of North America.

The rufous hummingbird holds the record for long distance travel in a year. They migrate over 2,500 miles (4,023 km) from Mexico through the west and up to Alaska, arriving in the North in late April or early May and staying until mid-August.

Migrating hummers face many dangers from the sudden changes of weather in the mountains. One rufous hummingbird was caught by an early winter because it remained in Alaska too long. An emergency air lift was arranged by the Hummingbird Rescue Center of California. A biologist caught the hummer in a garage in Alaska and got on the plane with the bird, feeding it every twenty-five minutes. After an "instant migration," it was released in California, where it could survive on its own.

In the Rocky Mountains, the broad-tailed hummingbird has a distinctive-sounding zing to its flight. Ranging into Canada, it is the most common of the four species in western mountains. Though they look much like the ruby-throated hummingbird and the black-chinned hummingbird, you can hear the difference.

One of the best places to see wild hummingbirds is in Ramsey Canyon, Arizona, at the Mile-HI Nature Conservancy wildlife preserve. More than thirteen species of hummers can be seen in the summer. Several species move into the United States, just north of the Mexican border after their breeding season in the Sierra Madre mountains of Mexico.

At the Sonora Desert Museum in Tucson, Arizona, the San Diego Zoo in California, and the Bronx Zoo in New York, hummers are exhibited in walk-through enclosures called aviaries. Zookeepers have tried to meet the difficult requirements of maintaining hummers in captivity so people can appreciate them close-up. The largest collection of stuffed hummingbirds is in the Fairbanks Museum in St. Johnsbury, Vermont. Over 113 species are present with 400 hummers on exhibit in this beautiful old museum.

There is nothing like seeing hummingbirds from your own window in your house. Because any patch of

A bird feeder filled with sugar water will attract
wild hummingbirds around your own home.

red flowers is likely to have an inquisitive hummer make a visit, planting certain flowers will help attract them. Fuschia (a shrub with red drooping flowers), firecracker plants, columbines, and bottle-brush shrubs, all produce large amounts of nectar-bearing flowers and will, in time, attract hummers.

You can also draw them close to home with bird feeders. Fill your hummingbird feeder with four parts water and one part sugar. Red food coloring, however, is not necessary and may harm the birds. If birds spend the winter, especially in Arizona and California, food must be provided all year. Be sure to change the sugar water if it gets moldy. If bottles remain empty for a time, hummers may look elsewhere for a steady supply and risk starving to death before they find a new food source.

To provide nesting materials, place lint from the dryer and cotton fluff outside. A source of moving water may also help a hummingbird population get established in your backyard. Of course, controlling

A baby hummingbird takes a drink of water from a human bird feeder.

your outdoor cats is a must because they are also very interested in hummingbirds.

Hummingbirds are special creatures that can grow comfortable around people, if they feel safe. Once you see them up close, you will want to help them survive by feeding them and making their frantic lives just a little bit easier.

FOR FURTHER READING

Anderson, Peter. *John James Audubon: Wildlife Artist.* New York: Franklin Watts, 1995.

Burnie, David. *Bird.* New York: Knopf Books for Young Readers, 1988.

Burton, Maurice. *Birds.* New York: Facts on File, 1985.

Foster, Susan Q. *The Hummingbird Among the Flowers.* Milwaukee, Wis.: Gareth Stevens, 1989.

Greenewalt, Crawford H. *Hummingbirds.* New York: Dover, 1990.

Harris, Alan, ed. *Birds.* New York: Dorling Kindersley, 1993.

Murray, Peter. *Hummingbirds.* Plymouth, Minn.: Childs World, 1993.

Tyrrell, Esther Q. *Hummingbirds: Jewels in the Sky.* New York: Crown Books for Young Readers, 1992.

INDEX

Italicized page numbers refer to illustrations.

ABOUT
THE
AUTHOR

Mark J. Rauzon is an environmental consultant and a writer-photographer who travels widely. He has worked as a biologist for the U.S. Fish and Wildlife Service and served as chair of the Pacific Seabird Group. Mr. Rauzon is the author of several children's books about animals, including *Parrots*, *Seabirds*, and *Vultures* for Franklin Watts. He lives in Oakland, California.